How To Find All Missing Persons / Unsolved Cases. And Collect All Reward Offers. Volume XXXXV. THE CASE OF JOANNE SHEEN-SMITH

DAVID GOMADZA

www.twofuture.world

How To Find All Missing Persons / Unsolved Cases. And Collect All Reward Offers. Volume XXXXV THE CASE OF JOANNE SHEEN-SMITH

Copyright © 2024 David Gomadza

All rights reserved.

Paperback ISBN: 9798328906661

How To Find All Missing Persons / Unsolved Cases. And Collect All Reward Offers. Volume XXXXV THE CASE OF JOANNE SHEEN-SMITH

DEDICATION

To a better future.

How To Find All Missing Persons / Unsolved Cases. And Collect All Reward Offers. Volume XXXXV THE CASE OF JOANNE SHEEN-SMITH

How To Find All Missing Persons / Unsolved Cases. And Collect All Reward Offers. Volume XXXXV THE CASE OF JOANNE SHEEN-SMITH

CONTENTS

How To Find All Missing Persons / Unsolved Cases.
And Collect All Reward Offers. Volume XXXXV.
THE CASE OF JOANNE SHEEN-SMITH 1
Afterlife Conversation.

and The Court Of Creation.   6

The Killers.   15

How To Find All Missing Persons / Unsolved Cases. And Collect All Reward Offers. Volume XXXXV THE CASE OF JOANNE SHEEN-SMITH

How To Find All Missing Persons / Unsolved Cases. And Collect All Reward Offers. Volume XXXXV THE CASE OF JOANNE SHEEN-SMITH

ACKNOWLEDGMENTS

Tomorrow's World Order

How To Find All Missing Persons / Unsolved Cases. And Collect All Reward Offers. Volume XXXXV THE CASE OF JOANNE SHEEN-SMITH

How To Find All Missing Persons / Unsolved Cases. And Collect All Reward Offers. Volume XXXXV THE CASE OF JOANNE SHEEN-SMITH

How To Find All Missing Persons / Unsolved Cases. And Collect All Reward Offers. Volume XXXXV. THE CASE OF JJOANNE SHEEN-SMITH

BACKGROUND INFORMATION

https://crimestoppers-uk.org/news-campaigns/news/2022/sep/we-offer-20-000-reward-in-bid-to-find-missing-southampton-mother-of-three

we are offering a reward of up to £20,000 for information on the disappearance of joanne sheen, who was last seen in southampton in december 2019.

44-year-old joanne, known as 'jo' and 'little jo', is described as being white, around 5ft 1in tall with a slim build. when last seen, she had long dark brown hair. joanne has a number of tattoos including a heart-and-dagger on her right upper arm and a band of flowers. she also has a tattoo of flowers on her right thigh and a star on her right foot. she has a tattoo of blue flowers on her left arm

hampshire constabulary are now treating her disappearance as a murder investigation but are keeping an open mind as to what happened to her.

the last corroborated sighting of joanne was on thursday, 5 december 2019, when she was travelling from fareham back to southampton with a friend.

there have been other unconfirmed sightings of joanne before christmas 2019 in the southampton area.

over the last two years, police have spoken to hundreds of witnesses and conducted several searches across southampton. the most recent was in july this year near mayflower park.

crimestoppers – which is independent of the police - is supporting this investigation by offering a reward of up to £20,000 for information we exclusively receive – either online or by calling freephone 0800 555 111 – that leads to the arrest and conviction of anyone linked to the murder of joanne sheen or the recovery of her body

Joanne Sheen was 44 when she was reported missing by her family on February 22 2020.

She was last seen when travelling from Fareham to Southampton with a friend on December 5 2019.

Four years on since the last sighting of Joanne, police have searched a flat in Southampton.

Speaking on the latest search in Parsonage Road, a spokesperson from Hampshire Police said: "Officers conducting enquiries into the disappearance of Joanne Sheen in November 2019 have carried out a warrant at an address on Parsonage Road in connection with their investigation.

How To Find All Missing Persons / Unsolved Cases. And Collect All Reward Offers. Volume XXXXV THE CASE OF JOANNE SHEEN-SMITH

TOMORROW'S WORLD ORDER'S PERSPECTIVES

USE OF PREDEFINED AFTERLIFE PARAMETERS

These guide souls the moment it exist the human body on its journey to Yahweh the creator these define what to do and what to expect as you go to hell or heaven if a souk leaves earth it enters ozone orbit and instantly everything reboots for it to start a new phase of life after living the earth's body now what happens is that it enters the ozone orbit and a simply click caused by the sudden drop of pressure from -1186 to – 20 means the bottom shaft of the soul will lift rapidly and this pushes its back into the air higher than its head best example is a penguin but with real human legs and head just the shape now God created a life predefined program for them instead of asking what should I do and where should I go they instantly know from predefined stencils if you did well and talked most about God then heaven is for you if you did evil and talked more about the devil then the devil is yours now if we Ask what can be of humans without souks this is the answer dead forever your soul is you a new transformation to the electromagnetic waves life where you see Yahweh for the first time and praise him and wish you had seen him a long time ago because of his Majesty and will always be there forever now what are all these you may ask these are rules to be guided by in the creation court in short it has everything humans know about the judges and the presiding judge who will always be Yahweh and 84 angels surrounding the altar 28 high priests who always say Yahweh have mercy on humans and 74 smaller courts priests who always say Yahweh has mercy on humans and 96 princesses who say glory to Yahweh forever and ever amen we have 96 elders who always say if I can why he can't meaning if the devil can drink blood why can't Yahweh who created the devil and blood do the same now this is not the same as saying if the devil can kill why can Yahweh its more on professional grounds rather than challenging now if we look at the inside of the court we have 81 priests surrounding the altar who say Yahweh be merciful to humans

but if they disobey you we put hem on trial for you and kill them for you almighty Yahweh inside this is a round circle where Yahweh sits and asks questions now if we look deep inside the court you will see that there are other things that resemble earth high courts like benches and chairs 10 times human sizes for the gods who are so enormous 2 are equal to 84 billion humans in size
predefined parameters for humans after death as in know what is inside is a large size of books the book of creation is among them with 10897867892836789012348678901245861789011 pages and is divided into humans first then chapter for animals then a chapter for angles then a chapter for gods and a chapter for Joseph Yahweh's best friend and a chapter for Yahweh's best friend's wife Anna and a chapter for Yahweh's wife Catitighit and lastly a chapter for Yahweh and recently a chapter for davidgomadza as Yahweh's representative on earth marking the new beginnings starting in 2025

1. tell us who killed you
   2. tell us what killed you
   3. tell us why and who killed you
   4. tell us why you died
   5. tell us what could have been done and is not done
   6. tell us what could be and why
   7. tell is when this happened
   8. tell us why this is so
   9. tell us why this is so
   10. what can be done to improve this

What does the book of creation say about davidgomadza David Gomadza is the first and last ruler to be appointed by Yahweh fir the next 25 billion years and will act as his representative on earth deciding cases and upholding his principles on earth and as such has been entitled to 489 trillion dollars in assets this number signifies eternity among humans and the beginning of a new Era chapter 7867892802893862841890287689018320867890123486789018236 487289128610 Creation manual the new Era of new electromagnetic wave conduit signed and dated by Yahweh himself on 27may2024 at 237800 Yatime
creation.universe.ya.start.end.find.davidgomadza.ya.askya.ya

Ask.read.creation.manucreation.universe.ya.start.end.find.davidgoma
askya.ya

Ask.rulesofthecourt.start.now.start
David Gomadza welcome the rules of court are guiding principles that tell you what to do and how to do it first you must always say I believe in the court of creation and I shall abide by he rules of this court and shall always do things according to the rules of this court in deciding the cases I am assigned to you must ask what can be done so that you know all your options before making choices the court system will make it easy to check files and ask the outcomes of the decision ask the court the final decision in any case.

THE AFTERLIFE CONVERSATION AND THE COUNCIL OF CREATION'S ANAYLSIS.

joanne sheen she left the house in the morning and found a friend waiting for her at the gate and said how can we be of help to each other i want your expertise and you want my charm so let's go we will be back after a while if you like she said okay i have been thinking about you anyway and said i can if you can she said okay we can see what to do and he lifted his hand and hit her with a huge hammer and carried her into his car and drove off to his house where he literally dragged her inside the house and sexually attacked her for hours and when she come around she said who t happened why am i naked and he said i can if you can i want sex with a half conscious woman those awake keep complaining that i am big and to stop i am tired of that i prefer a dead woman and i want just to keep going and until i cum that's what is sex all over this cum outside this and that is bullshit okay so don't ask let's do again and she screamed help help then he said no one live around me so relax and let's enjoy this moment together shall we and he took a bottle of gin and said i can if you can but what can we do together i think you want me to do you when you are dead that is not a problem just keep doing that we are friends it's not like you don't know me so what is this about she said i did not agree you force me to have sex with you that is a crime and he said it's a crime because you want and i don't want he said what can i do that you can't do and he sat down and said i want to but it's all about you and not me did you ask me what i want and he said yes i said if i can you too so it's your turn knock me out and have sex with me too then she said okay and took a hammer and tried to hit him in the head and he said i can't if you can't then he said we can make a deal i think you want only when you are dead then let it be and took the hammer and struck her hard that she instantly died and he said i told you you want it when you are dead and he had sex with her and took her to his car and drove off in the woods and said i can if you can but i can't get caught because she agreed she was supposed to say no then i know that she doesn't want then i can say if i could then but she said okay and then this is okay as such the task is completed and we can move on and say if i can then you can but so i hide her coordinates are 38.6789028 and 30.981289024 in southampton near alfred motors i can see their garage as i bury her but i am on the other side of the road and it's written that only heavy vehicles and he laughed and said what's heavy about her maybe she carry shit because women who don't like sex carry a lot of shit and he stumped on her belly and spinned around and started digging the grave and said i can if you can but he you can if i can and put her in the shallow grave and said what is to be is to be you are destined to die so death is a solution for you and said what can be said about you and me disaster because you ended up dead but then again what else is there between a sex maniac and someone who doesn't want sex nothing but death so death it is and i don't lie i tell you straight fuck and go or rot forever it's that simple but all women don't understand until i slide then in a grave instead of their vaginas but i must as the creator made us hungry all the time when all women refuse so what can we do you answer that one until you solve this women will keep dying i rest my case before you god

my name is aspen doregall i was born on 27 april 1967 i am going to tell you a story you won't believe i love sex i think there is nothing i have enjoyed the most as sex i am well endowed and that means sex is the vest that can be imagine penetrating a vagina and cummings inside and the woman smiling that is life but i have had the greatest problem because i can't find a woman who can satisfy me when they are alive all complain and it's all about my size when i was growing up i thought big size means getting laid all the time until i hit puberty then found out that i really can't get laid all i had was attention that's all i talk to my friend he had sex a the time and me i rarely and one day i asked god to create a woman with a big vagina for me and someone said try arse and laughed so i became very violent towards women then i realised that arse is just the same with the smells then i decided to find women who want sex when they were asleep but not even one then last year i met this one joanne sheen she said sex is good if a man is well endowed then i flattered and showed my penis she said oh that's what i am talking about then we had sex several times but the last time vagina literally dropped it opened so much that i need two of these put together then she started to say i need even bigger than that and i said we can try arse as well and we tried and that fell too then she said i can't anymore what else can drop to the ground like that no one touch me all run away so i am technically you so you should feel proud you sold me your problem but i am a woman i put anything there it's easy the other day i put a doll and put all inside and she laughed i cringed with rage then she left before anything and i was gutted that was 8 months ago on 2 september 2020 then i had here and there but all briefly so i don't show she just discover then say i am going to the loo and that's it she put all clothes there and run away saying take the money o never get laid again if all rings fall

joanne sheen said what can i do today if i can then maybe i can go to the park and relax but i want to get things back in form with aspen but he ruined everything all rims literally fell off and its just some sagging something i can't call it a vagina anymore and everything drops literally i have to wear thick underwear all the time but now i have no one but him so tonight i can make it up with him and say finish it off i might as well agree to that because he ruined me i think there is a woman out there who can live without a vagina and as i was just thinking about him he turned up and said what can we do i can if you can then i said okay and the next thing i know was that i was in his house in an area out of nowhere in the village part of southampton to a city called eres outside of southampton about a mile driving then he said i can if you can but you and now it's your turn i felt rage and he said use the hammer too and make love to me and said how can i penetrate you but he said you don't have to just ogle this monster and i said it ruined me maybe i ruin it as well then he grabbed the hammer and struck so hard on the left temple that i died instantly i only heard a long ago and something started moving fast inside my body shouting time countdown from 8 seconds until it's 1 then i blacked out and woke up at the reception in hell with so many people all dead i counted about 800000 waiting to be served and ever since i am still there waiting to be seen by god himself i heard he has 8 heads and move like a coach back and forth that alone is scary but i can deal with that

aspen maerop

i think today might be a great sex day because i want to but i think if i convince her then she can agree what can i do big destroys everything all i need is sex but how on earth can i fulfill that no one likes me it's just hard to believe i used to boast so much that i am a god when it comes to sex then after my own girlfriend said everything is ruined i never had any one ask me for sex my friend an average guy women ask him for sex in front of me and it hurts like hell because of size i want sex all the time then what can i do if they all refuse maybe kill i thought one day one time use but enjoy to the max and dispose of so tonight i promised myself if she can't say yes i take her to god for two reasons

1. she keep on telling other women that i ruined her and show everyone that sagging thing i can even call it a vagina
2. she keep accusing me that once you go aspen then that's it you will never have sex again in all its glory even arse she shit herself all the time now imagine a life like that she says

now all i have to do is ask her a question she say yes if not then carry her here dead or alive and have great sex and bury her in the woods here in southampton where no one knows i need to mark the place so that this becomes the start of the great sex adventure

pc aners openser said sitting in his office the big is becoming wild now because starvation is breeding a monster in him something we want so we have cases that can't be solved for decades then rip the benefits at the end in bonus as the fund reaches a whooping one

million that is if god don't ruin our plan and say return all that you filthy bastards and he laugh had and threw up then heard aspen on the speaker cursing that he is so big and begging god to create a woman for him with a big vagina and laughed had and said louder pressing the button so that aspen hears this and said why not try arse and giggled that he heard that and instantly another officer parse said what's so fun you seem to laugh to yourself nowadays and he said no sir just checking how my vocabulary can be humorous and handed him the aspen file and said he can create cases that are hard to solve for a billion years even god will struggle to figure out what had just happened he said okay but we don't work in reverse okay if people hear you talk like that then we look like crooks on heat worse than prostitutes because we have duties to prevent all from this and not to encourage this for early retirement imagine if a the president is to know that we swindle government money into our private bank accounts surely we will all be dismissed and put in jail but then again it's hard to prove unless god is here even if he is here i don't think he waste time snooping on us rather than on saving the world
aspen maerop
if there was a god surely he had given me a normal size dick so that i marry and settle down imagine with a wife i can fuck all night like my friend bill but i guess it's punishment for me so i have to give god a reason and start killing all my these women one by one until they are all dead if i go to god i will say i killed all because no one wants to fuck and all are one timers after that i am on my own he looked in his tool box and took a huge steel hammer and practiced to hit harder and smiled and covered it with a shirt written if i can then you can then put it into his car in the groove box and said if i can then you can but if i have to then must do it right i need a shovel in the back as well and laughed imagine killing and dumping the body anywhere how will that last and thought about it and said i can't get caught though otherwise it will be a lose and he started thinking about the other man who made noises and said am i losing it or what and checked everywhere for bugs and left and pretended to have gone and stood behind the door and listened but there was nothing then he left heading to number 84 astert street whistling and touching his mr big and smiled sex or death i work for the devil now if anyone has to

ask this is me in my life and another in my life where i make the commands sex all night or death its that simple and he said what can be of tonight i pray to god to soften her heart she is the only woman who agreed in my entire life that's 49 years of sexual active life that's so sad i cry sometimes he said if i can't get laid tonight I made my mind i bury her and move in her house she showed me her papers for the house asking me to marry her but she was old for me then then things changed she found a younger man and said you chose me because i liked you and refused me because of age so today i refuse you because of age not because of sex and left and for 8 months i wank and she sent me a text message today and it reads i need you tonight let's work something out i have a house i can add you so we move it together what do you say its all paid for i had a good job and paid all by age 50 from the age of 24 but it was hard i turned everyone for the house my mother had no house and i have no kids it's funny huh so tonight let's make up and move in together so we can be together i love you aspen marop she always call me wrong surname my surname is maerop but when she writes she write marop but it's all good i checked the value of the house it looks like the range of 2million that can be an incentive bury her and everything and take the house too sell it and go abroad for 10 years 2 mill is enough he smiled and said everything must play right for me and we ask what is that i need from life god gave me a big and a brain as we i might use this strength to rich myself from a woman who thinks i ruined her anywhere he smiled and left

pc aers said tonight something is going on but i will keep a low profile and follow this beast and see where it goes and say hey what do we have here but look from afar and see what he is up to then he had a phone call from his wife who said come home

i am melissa surge who is married to pc aers but written with a p at the beginning paers who always criticize sex meaning the ay i like it as to how i give it he says i can fuck he wants it all night but forget he get peanuts at work to avoid luxury but said i will make it to you when we are old and then i say what the point as you will give it to others you will be old and curse and say i can quit tomorrow if it wasn't for my daughter mellisa as we who is now 6 years old if i ask what is the future mellisa can be married to the president of this

country and he laughs and say that will be something
he then left in his ford mondeo reg 87pt ser then drove like a lunatic o retaking before he said what can i do for you if i can then you can then he said i will but instantly took something from the grove box and struck her hard in broad daylight and said if i can you can yes is the answer anything else will result in death but i did not kill you just give you a lesson so that when you wake up you make the right choice he then drove at speed running to have sex fingerings her vagina he then got her out of the car dragging her without worrying to be seen he then slammed the door and said i can if you can then entered the house then said i wi if you can then she said what then sat down naked and fluid coming out of her big vagina and cursed and said i was going to let you anywhere why hit me first and he said smiling i can if you can you didn't say yes that why you got the hammer and laughed jokingly she looked lost and said aspen listen to me this was my idea so what can be a problem after that why do you have to do that i thought we have an agreement to move in together i have house papers with me look living together she took house papers and threw at him he picked them up and read them joanne sheen-smith and said 20 january 1986 southampton and smiled again and said so you were once married to a smith she said yes but he died in a car accident in 1990 on 3rd december and he smiled and said so where is his life insurance money and she smiled and said if we talk then i can then she dressed up and he looked furious and said we haven't started you were asleep i did one that meant to start things out between us and fuck a night she said okay where is my phone i make a call to the police so they know we are alright and not to come and he said what why would they come anywhere how did you call them with your phone vagina and laughed he said she said you call them all the time they told me you want to kill me for the house and i told them that i marry him and leave the house with him as i am older do you know that it's them who want my house for capital gains tax since when a police officer come to your house and say when you sell the house we want capital gains tax this morning pc atertop said i will come to check when you se the house before that monster kill you and put his name on the house
i am pc aterts aterop i work for the southampton police and i am

aroused by capital gains tax i had no idea what it was about until a colleague said it is all about capital gains tax it's the retirement check we get all at the end and smiled i only knew what he was talking at at the end and i got an election literally because that means rich at the end and when asked if any ever get rich he said most retire way early in 40s because you stay in the end they will find out

he then said i can't if you can't then went out and said what can be done about all this if we are meant to get married what will be the use of a this when you can easily get everything for free i don't want to die so let this police man know we are all alright before he comes so i agreed and she said we are all right but we are having hammer sex so don't come with guns and shoot us otherwise we take you to the grave alive and bury you in a shallow one so listen carefully bye and laughed but no one said anything
pc aterops i don't understanding these rich people they ca us retarded until that day when they need help and say help me in code he has a hammer he actually used it once but don't come slow come fast because i had no idea he is violent the sex shook my brain so much i am dizzy so come with guns where in england they have guns she want me to be killed for asking for capital gains tax i pretend she didn't call and drag everything to hell with you but if i say that don't i get sacked and he instantly rung her but the phone was switched off and he sat down and call his boss pc atpomn who said i can't intervene in private matters unless he had refused her to call and he growled and said okay and sat on the couch and said i am paid to defend justice but today there might not be justice i can't believe i just sit down for her to be killed maybe it's the right thing the way she complains about him i said one day do you want him dead and she said if this happened to your wife would you let him live?
i can't live with my vagina ruined on top of that you start become violent why when we are talking about moving in together sometimes i don't understand you aspen i thought you were happy what do you want i am doing this for you you can have all this for free so what do you want what is wrong can we work this out if not then what can we do about this if you cant listen to me if i am helping you sit down when i am talking to you show me respect so

that i know i am doing this for you and he lifted his hand and hit her this time harder than before and instantly body alarms started going alarms started going on and said long ago started at 20.34pm 8 seconds left and instantly calculations started
breath 7
ast 10
aspen 9
as0 7
as8 10
as20 11
as14 19
as29 7
as7 0
as8 10
as8 20
as7 19
as2 10
as80 24
as74 91
as23 34
as10 0
and she breathed hard and died instantly her soul left through the window and he said he'll what is that hey where are you going don't be reporting me to god
soul
i ran out as the pig creature started saying death is coming fast get out then i breathed once and left so fast i nearly smashed the window and he said hey where are you going do t be reporting me to god and laughed holding a beer written cider
i had great sex tonight and again i will keep.enjoying i think this is the reason why i am doing this and make sure that i get that house and never to feel ashamed again but to enjoy life after that i will pay the next woman handsomely for ruining her vagina in advance so that she can't refuse after that i will become the real man i wanted but first thing is first sex and then bury her for good so that it i'll answer all the questions about the house then a knock at the door startled me and i said who is it then he said i am pc aterops open the door before

i smash it and i refused and said if you don't get out of my property i will kill you and give you the big one first and bury you or feed you to the pig that eats even your bones and he kicked the door but in frustration and i just get down and started making love to her as she started to spasm and i said if we had not fought we could have been a great couple because only you in my life agreed but then we faced to agree on critical things and that has resulted in death then after he took her to the forest in southampton just outside the city and dug a small grave and dig it out and buried her and said i can if you can but you failed to say yes and that alone has cost you your life but it's all good we meet again i believe now i saw the small duck running out of you i never killed anyone or been when someone died today i witnessed god that means i will follow you one day thanks for the house i changed that name already to aspen maertes for the first time in my life i own a house you deserve heaven bye my love until we meet again he was about to drive off when a car appeared and flashed him and he removed his pants and put them back on and pointed as if a gun and shoot the driver who drove off fast
coordinates
78.76829872
77.2876283867890
when he returned he sat down and started looking at the house papers and signed his full name aspen maertes margene and said we can be rich again if i sell this house fast then he drove off
the house was sold off the same night on 28 october 2021
i will sale it online for even half but cash and i sold it for 1.8million to a bank that buy and sell cash in bank the next day and spain here i come.
current coordinates are in spain

THE KILLERS THE CONFESSIONS AND THE COORDINATES

The killer uses the following names;

my name is aspen doregall i was born on 27 april 1967 i am going to tell you a story you won't believe i love sex i think there is nothing i

have enjoyed the most as sex i am well
aspen maerop
aspen marop

aspen maertes margene and said we can be rich again if i sell this house fast then he drove off
the house was sold off the same night on 28 october 2021
i will sale it online for even half but cash and i sold it for 1.8million to a bank that buy and sell cash in bank the next day and spain here i come.
current coordinates are in spain

He owned and drove s ford mondeo reg 87pt ser then drove like a lunatic

Joanne Sheen coordinates coordinates
78.76829872
77.2876283867890
 or
hide her coordinates are 38.6789028 and 30.981289024 in southampton near alfred motors i can see their garage as i bury her but i am on the other side of the road and it's written that only heavy vehicles and he laughed and said what's heavy about her

…I found God…visit www.twofuture.world

How To Find All Missing Persons / Unsolved Cases. And Collect All Reward Offers. Volume XXXXV THE CASE OF JOANNE SHEEN-SMITH

THE CLAIM

the reward offer

THE COLLECTION

www.twofuture.world/donate

ABOUT DAVID GOMADZA

visit www.twofuture.world

signed david gomadza
ask.davidgomadzaauthorised.licensed.checkya.askya.ya

19 June 2024 22.29 pm
scotland
00447719210295
davidgomadza@hotmail.com
info@twofuture.world

www.ingramcontent.com/pod-product-compliance
Lightning Source LLC
Chambersburg PA
CBHW032312240526
45464CB00023BA/2998